MICHELLE GIBERT

FOREWORD BY DETRICK L.GASKINS

REJECTION

"LIVING INSIDE OUT"

IDENTIFYING and HEALING from the spirit of rejection

MICHELLE GIBERT

FOREWORD BY DETRICK L.GASKINS

REJECTION

"LIVING INSIDE OUT"

IDENTIFYING and HEALING from the spirit of rejection

Dedication

The dedication of this book comes approximately one month after I begin writing. Many people dedicate books to their spouses, children, family, friends, and sometimes to those who have played a vital role in their spiritual growth; but this was different for me. I wanted to do some of that, and maybe all of that, but I was not able to. Throughout this process, I trusted God to lead me through every phase of writing this book, so I decided to do the same with the dedication, so I waited.

As I was refining chapter four, "Rejection and Relationships," there I had it; God had given it to me, my dedication. It was quite a bit strange, but if it's ok with God, it's ok with me.

I dedicate this book to every man I have ever dated, to every man that I have ever been in any type of relationship with, rather good or bad. I dedicate this book to the gang member, to the cheater, to the faithful, to the fathers of my children, and to the ex-husband. I dedicate this book to the men that had *no chance*, to the men that were dating the spirit of rejection. There weren't many of them as I was very withdrawn, but there were enough for me to know and understand after my deliverance that they never had a chance. It doesn't matter who and what they were, as I look back I understand who and what I was... So I dedicate this book to you!

Love is never an option when you're overcome with rejection; God is the only one that can fill that void.

Chapter Summary

Thank You

Foreword by Apostle Detrick L. Gaskins

Introduction 1

Thank You

Interceding With The Word Christian Center Intl. for all your love and support during this process. YOU'RE THE BEST!

Apostle Michelle Gibert

FOREWORD

Rejection *"Living Inside Out"*

Rejection is a root spirit. **Rejection** makes you hate being rejected but not trust in being loved. **Rejection** allows you to release love but makes it hard for you to receive it. **Rejection** keeps the mind in a mode of distrust. **Rejection** empowers our past to keep our present stagnated and our future unreachable without its permission. **Rejection** serves as the thorn and thistle of the prophetic grace to keep movement deactivated. **Rejection** shuts out the voice of God, so the wells of edification, comfort, and encouragement stay closed within the believer's life. Seemingly to some, there is no end to rejection's fury and or rule, yet I beg to differ.

In **Rejection** *"Living Inside Out"* Apostle Michelle Gibert passionately teaches us through the word of God and her own life experiences, how to *recognize*, *resist* and *renounce* the spirit of rejection and all its baggage. As you journey with her through her own tunnels of transition, moving beyond the crowded corridors of rejection's ruling armies of abandonment, fear, and hurt, you will see the end of your battle and that it's clearly more for you than against you.

Apostle Detrick L. Gaskins
Kairos International Training Center & Assembly
Orlando, FL.

Introduction

Let me start this introduction by saying, "the only permanent cure for rejection is and will always be *'The Love of God.'*"

Over the years from the time I can remember I have always searched for a way out of feeling rejected by people. I spent years living and feeling like an outsider in a very big world. As I look back at this place in my life, interestingly enough, I find that I was not alone in my search.

Rejection is a worldwide epidemic, a disease that has the potential to spread like cancer, without a cure.

There are many people that are suffering from rejection that are looking for a way out. When one has a root spirit of rejection, they spend an overwhelming amount of time and energy searching for remedies and in the end, come up with zero results. One of the reasons for this is they are actually looking to fill a void, an empty space in their lives that has been caused by some tragic event or a series thereof that only God can fill.

What makes this search a waste of valuable time; is time. The time you spend trying to fill this void through people, money and/or success, all while trying to feel good about yourself in the process.

In my case, from the time I was able to dress myself, I did just that, dressed myself; I covered up. I mean what people don't know can't hurt you right? Wrong. Wrong because rejection is not about other people, it's about you. Rejection has the ability to mask itself in the face of others because the face of others serves as a secure hiding place for the spirit of rejection, but it's really about you.

Rejections main course of action is to move you into a place of self-rejection and self-hatred, and if successful, you will *never* be able to walk in who God has called you to be, in fact, you will find yourself carrying around the spirit of rejection with you wherever you go, always feeling as if you're being rejected and never-ever accepted.

When you move into a place of self-rejection, your very thoughts become unstable and contaminated, leaving you in a place where you don't trust yourself or those around you.

Rejection causes you to look for love in all the wrong places, all while taking on projects of healing for people you believe to be worse off than you are so that you can feel good about yourself. Well, the

2

projects will fall apart, leaving you worse off than before you started.

In the pages of this book, you will begin to see how the spirit of rejection truly works like a well-designed system, a system that has been designed to break you down spiritually and emotionally, eventually becoming a part of your everyday walk.

1

Defining Rejection

I would like to say that defining rejection is an easy process, but I won't. Looking up rejection in the Webster's Dictionary is an easy process, googling rejection and/or taking from someone else's definition is an easy process; but defining rejection from personal experience requires the work of the Holy Spirit in you, which in turn, requires that you have *walked* through the mountains, the high places and low places of rejection, which can make defining rejection not only a tedious process but one that requires self-examination.

When it comes to defining rejection, I have become my own dictionary. God has allowed me, because of the knowledge He has given me where rejection is concerned, to not only define but to expose the spirit of rejection. Through my experiences, God has enabled me to deal with every element of rejection while bringing it to the forefront in detail.

Let us first take a look at how Webster's Dictionary defines rejection.

1a: *the action of rejecting: the state of being rejected. b: an immune response in which foreign tissue (as of a skin graft or transplanted organ) is attacked by immune system components of the recipient organism.*
2: *something rejected.*

When looking at the above definitions, I still have absolutely no idea what rejection means for me. So looking it up in the dictionary will in no way help you to heal and it will certainly not set you on the road to freedom. The one thing I do agree with is 1b; it most certainly launches an attack against your immune system having a tragic effect on your life.

You are able to define rejection when you can speak rejections language, when you have sought God as to the how, when, where and why this spirit became a part of your very being.

Now it's my turn. How would I define rejection?

1a: *a very dark spirit that comes to keep you in a dark place.*
1b: *a spirit that is released in the lives of God's creation which brings forth self-hatred.*
1c: *a STRONG MAN that is determined to take over your very identity.*

2a: *a demonic system that is designed to break down all Godly traits, rendering you helpless and leaving you victim to the world.*

When looking at rejection from a Spiritual standpoint, you can most certainly see the difference in the definitions. While one is Holy Spirit revealed through experience, releasing God-given revelation, the other is naturally and scientifically based.

Many people suffer (*to experience pain, illness, or injury: to experience something unpleasant (such as defeat, loss or damage): to become worse because of being badly affected by something*) from rejection and have yet to find a way out.

The word suffer may appear to be a bit harsh to use, as it indicates affliction, but it is accurate and appropriate where the spirit of rejection is concerned. The internal and external breakdown that the spirit of rejection causes in one's life over time is massive.

As we journey together through the pages of this book you will find and begin to define rejection for yourself, and as you do, you will begin to feel the veil of deception being removed from your eyes. The more you can see the freer you will be.

Therefore if the Son makes you free, you shall be free indeed (John 8:36). NKJV

2

My Midnight
"Experience in the Birth Canal"

T he birth canal is of significance as we know in the birthing process; without the birth canal there is no passageway for delivery. In the delivery process, there's an opening of the cervix into the birth canal during labor and birth. The baby travels through the cervix down the birth canal and through the vaginal opening into the world where life begins.

When looking at the birthing process, you must also take into consideration genealogy: *(the study of family history; the history of a particular family showing how the different members of the family are related to each other).* In this place, you will find the dynamics', the inner workings of that family; you find bloodline blessings and curses alike.

The creation process in itself is very supernatural, as well as the forming of the child in the womb. In this process, there is a supernatural encounter that takes place between the emotional state of the mother and the child. The child not only takes on the feelings and emotions of the mother but being formed through the natural bloodline (DNA) of both parents, the child is also subject to the different spirits of the parents rather good or bad. This is a process that is repeated from generation to generation, therefore, with each birth, a new generation is being born.

From Generation to Generation

Every spirit has a *point of entry;* a time in which that particular spirit entered a person's life. This is very important where deliverance is concerned, as it reveals how long that particular spirit has been present. Consider Jesus' encounter with the father of the boy possessed by an impure spirit and His question posed to the father.

> So they brought him. When the **spirit saw** Jesus, it immediately threw the boy into a convulsion. He fell to the ground and rolled around, foaming at the mouth.

> Jesus asked the boy's father, **"How long has he been like this?"**

> **"From childhood,"** he answered (Mark 9:20-21).
> Emphasis added.

10

As God began to take me through the process of deliverance, I found that the spirit of rejection had come down from generation to generation; it had become a family trait.

When a spirit travels down several generations it becomes hidden; it becomes the norm for the family. When something becomes the norm, people stop looking at it no matter how damaging it is. This is where ungodly spirits gain strength and become successful in their intended assignment.

Dark spirits are more effective when you are in the dark; when you have on a blindfold, because you cannot fight against that which you cannot see. Behind the scenes, because it becomes the norm for the family, the spirit (whatever it is) attempts to destroy everything in its path, and I was in its path.

On the outside, everything looked good and well put together. Looking through the *natural* eye you would never know the pain I was suffering on the inside. There was no clear view for the naked eye to see my rejection. Not only was the rejection hidden, but I was hidden and hidden well (like so many), I was living *INSIDE OUT*.

Experiencing rejection one after another, constantly feeling alone, late nights crying out to God asking for His help, all while blinded to the why and having absolutely no idea why I was living a life of internal dysfunction, were the very thoughts that were tormenting me. As I sought God for answers placing the emotions and feelings of rejection I was having before Him, it felt as though I was hurting more because God was bringing to the surface things that had been buried for so very long.

He reveals the deep things of darkness and brings deep shadows into the light (Job 12:22).

One of the biggest misconceptions concerning healing and deliverance is that you don't have to deal with the hidden stuff. Contrary to popular belief, *"you do."* How does something come out without first coming up? When coming out you will experience some discomfort, and in some cases, pain as the Holy Spirit reveals the point of entry. This is a place where God goes deep and scrapes the very root of your soul, the place of healing, deliverance, and cleansing.

he saved us, not because of righteous things we had done, but because of his mercy. He saved us through the washing of rebirth and renewal by the Holy Spirit, (Titus 3:5).

There is absolutely nothing we can do to bring healing and deliverance to our own souls, except to surrender to the work of the Holy Spirit.

I had been searching and interrogating myself for years trying to get free. I was fighting myself for myself and I was losing. It was almost like hitting a brick wall over and over again continuing to be scarred, yet having no bandages. I was working overtime trying to heal myself on my own without God.

This self-searching behavior in itself is destructive and does not work. Trying to figure out rejection (or any spirit) and its origin without God, is not only difficult but damaging and next to impossible. Any form of deliverance without God can and will cause more harm than good, and that's what was happening.

On the inside I was self-destructing, but in no way could I show that on the outside, so I set a great routine for myself that I believed would protect me from the outside world of rejection, not realizing that it was in me.

I lived in my own little world, hiding in the very mountains of my home trying to build my own little family, which caused me to make decisions in relationships that were bringing me to my own demise. I could see it, but I could in no way afford to let it go; *thinking*, this just might be the relationship that will fill whatever emptiness I'm feeling and/or complete the love I so very need in my life. Of course, this was not the case, but I was in no way ever going to stop my (ungodly) search for love without God.

Rejection the Strong man

I was bound, unable to move. I was being held down by something so much stronger than I was. Not only did I not know back then that rejection was a strong man, but I had no idea what a strong man was at the time. The spirit of rejection had taken possession of my house and called it its own, I had lost complete control.

According to Webster's Dictionary, the word strong means *having great power and ability: having a lot of strength: not easy to break or damage.*

The above definition most certainly describes the strength and ability of a strong man. When a strong man is present you always feel as if you are in a fight for your life, because you are.

The assignment of a strong man is to chain you down and to keep you from moving forward, causing you to become ineffective in many different areas of your life.

Because the fight is a spiritual one, only the power of God can get you up from this place. Without the power of God, you will be rendered helpless, causing yourself more harm than good. Fighting in the flesh (without God) weakens you spiritually, causing natural depression. You become tired and worn out easily because you're fighting spiritual powers without Spiritual Power.

"When a strong man, fully armed, guards his own house, his possessions are safe. But when someone stronger attacks and overpowers him, he takes away the armor in which the man trusted and divides up his plunder* (Luke 11:21-22).
Emphasis added.

This is exactly what a strong man does. He comes to take full possession of a house and when he does he calls it his own. Although we are able to tie up the strong man *(Mark 3:27),* we are unable to do this without the power of God working within us.

You, dear children, are from God and have overcome them, because the one who is in you is greater than the one who is in the world (1 John 4:4).

The healing process can only begin when the strong man is tied up and stripped of his armor. A strong man trusts his armor, he trusts it to protect and cover him, so when it is removed he is open for eviction. His cover (armor) can be *pride, anger, resentment, shyness, etc.*, therefore it must be taken away (exposed), and once taken away he is weakened and destroyed.

> *But everything exposed by the light becomes visible—and everything that is illuminated becomes a light* (Ephesians 5:13).

The different layers of armor are revealed through prayer by the Holy Spirit. Discernment *(to perceive directly: have direct cognition of; to have understanding of: to recognize the nature of: discern)*, gives us the ability to see the strong man's armor manifested in one's character, but because of a lack of knowledge we as God's children don't look beyond the surface.

The Word of God teaches that *"we are destroyed for a lack of knowledge* (Hosea 4:6)." What we don't know can and will destroy us.

Many times due to a lack of knowledge, we as humans tend to protect our root. We cover our pain, not realizing that we are protecting the strong man; that we are providing the armor for the very darkness God desires to deliver us from. *Pride, anger, rebellion, etc.*, are all coverings for the strong man working at the root.

16

In fact, no one can enter a strong man's house without first tying him up. Then he can plunder the strong man's house (Mark 3:27).

Rejection is a STRONG MAN, fully armed, ready for battle, guarding the very house in which he has occupied for so very long.

Like any evil spirit, it takes the power of God in you to free you; again, this is not something you are able to do on your own. It is God and God only that brings healing and deliverance to the broken soul of man. We lose battles when we fight on our own.

My Midnight My Best Night

After they had been severely flogged, they were thrown into prison, and the jailer was commanded to guard them carefully. When he received these orders, he put them in the inner cell and fastened their feet in the stocks.

About midnight Paul and Silas were praying and singing hymns to God, and the other prisoners were listening to them. Suddenly there was such a violent earthquake that the foundations of the prison were shaken. At once all the prison doors flew open, and everyone's chains came loose (Acts 16:25-26).

The above scripture verses are very profound when it comes to deliverance. I chose this particular passage of scripture because not only does it speak to my midnight experience, but it speaks to the magnitude of the chains that had me bound and to the power of God that released me from those chains.

Rather we realize it or not, we have been incarcerated, thrown in jail, and imprisoned when we are in bondage to any ungodly spirit. We are flogged, handcuffed and chained down. In this place it's difficult to move, it's difficult to live because you are bound with chains too strong for human hands to break. You are rendered helpless.

After continually seeking God for answers, and feeling extremely lonely inside, I came to the end of my rope in 1997.

One night after spending time worshipping and praising God, I found myself stretched out across the foot of my bed at *midnight* still fully dressed as if I had somewhere to go, praying and crying out to God. I once again begin to ask God *why* the rejection was so bad in my life. I remember saying, *"God, what is it?"*

Very gently, as I know my Father to be in the healing process, I heard a soft, quiet voice say, *"When your mother was pregnant with you they wanted to abort you,"* the Lord continued, *"they had many conversations about it."* At that very moment, I begin to cry uncontrollably. I felt the rejection rise to the very height in which it was released into my life. I felt as if I were back in the womb traveling through the very birth canal that did not want me, not only was I devastated, but I was hurt. The cry was so uncontrollable that I knew that there was a groundbreaking going on inside of me.

Strangely enough, as I was being broken, I was also being placed back together again. In all the hurt and pain that I was feeling as I was going through this process, I also felt the comfort and love of God come upon me. It was almost as if the Lord took me in His arms and began to rock me. It was at this point that the Lord begins to speak with me yet again. Through all the crying, I heard the Lord say, *"Now forgive your mother."* After crying more, I said *"I forgive her,"* and at that moment I did.

As God continued to take me through the deliverance process, He begins to reveal my mother's own rejection to me (from generation to generation), which humbled my heart and the healing process had begun.

Suddenly there was such a violent earthquake that the foundations of the prison were shaken. At once, all the prison doors flew open, and everyone's chains came loose (Acts 16:26).

When a strong man is evicted by the power of God from the very home he'd inhabited for so long he puts up a fight; there is a groundbreaking that takes place. My very foundation was shaken, the root of rejection was pulled up and the doors of the prison *flew* open. Chains were loosed and I was free. It was an experience like no other.

Being overwhelmed by the presence of God, the next day I called my mother and father and asked them both, and they both confirmed, *yes*. My dad wanted to know how I knew; I don't remember ever answering his question as it no longer mattered.

MY MIDNIGHT WAS MY BEST NIGHT. The point of entry was finally revealed and the axe was laid to the root of rejection.

Although I was free I now had work to do. I had lived a life of rejection in which I had become accustomed to; it had become a way of life for me.

God revealed the point of entry and the jail cell was now opened, but now I had to learn how to walk, I had to learn how to live. God had to teach me how to deal with the spirit of mind-control that had come upon me; He had to teach me how to escape the control of others.

When overcome with rejection you become a target for the spirit of control because you always feel as though you always have to please. This feeling comes from a place of needing to be accepted. Rejection serves as a magnet for the spirit of control.

As we continue to identify the inner workings of the spirit of rejection, it will become increasingly clear that in many instances your need to be loved takes precedence over everything else in your life. The axe was laid to the root, but now the blood of Jesus had to be applied.

Time and time again, I have seen people go through the deliverance process and never do what it takes to remain free. Working out your salvation is a process. Laying the axe to the root is the beginning of that process, but now you have the responsibility of maintaining your freedom and working out your own salvation.

Therefore, my dear friends, as you have always obeyed—not only in my presence, but now much more in my absence—continue to work out your salvation with fear and trembling, for it is God who works in you to will and to act in order to fulfill his good purpose (Philippians 2:12-13).

You have been purposed on purpose and everything Satan attempts is designed to keep you from walking out that purpose.

*"Before I formed you in the womb I knew you,
before you were born I set you apart; I appointed
you as a prophet to the nations (Jeremiah 1:5)."*

In order to maintain your deliverance; Church is necessary, reading and studying the Word of God is necessary, praise and worship is necessary, and accountability are all necessary.

When an impure spirit goes out of a person and finds no rest, it goes back to that person; the house in which it inhabited for so long. If you have not done the necessary work and your house is unoccupied by the Word of God, you are open for not only the root to grow back, but for the entry of other evil spirits as well.

*"When an impure spirit comes out of a person, it
goes through arid places seeking rest and does not
find it. Then it says, 'I will **return to the house I
left.'** When it arrives, it finds the house
unoccupied, swept clean and put in order. Then it
goes and takes with it seven other spirits more
wicked than itself, and they go in and live there.
And the final condition of that person is worse than
the first. That is how it will be with this wicked
generation (Matthew 12:43-45)."* Emphasis added.

3

Rejections Only Mission

There are many misconceptions concerning the spirit of rejection, which is why it's taking double the time needed for people to get free. People simply need to know the truth. We need to get to the bottom-line of rejections *only* mission, which will speed up the process of healing and deliverance.

When people are able to see the truth blinders are removed. Skirting around the truth will never set people free; it will only cause people to wrestle internally with not knowing, which will have long-lasting external effects.

Then you will know the truth, and the truth will set you free (John 8:32).

Many times when we look at rejection, we look at people and how they treat us; we place or focus on their likes, dislikes and actions concerning us, but we neglect to see that this is a strategic move on behalf of the enemy. We never pay attention to the fact that they are merely being used to keep the spirit of rejection alive and active in our lives. People are not the cause, root, problem or source; Satan is.

Rejection like any other evil spirit has a birthplace (a place in which that particular spirit took root), and although we know that in Christ Jesus, every evil spirit also has a place of death, we must allow the redemptive work of the cross to take us through the process of healing and deliverance.

Throughout the years the more I felt rejected the more I rejected myself. This is rejections only mission; *"to cause you to reject yourself; 'to cause you to walk in self-hatred,' and 'low self-esteem,'"* and Satan will use whatever and whoever is open to accomplish his mission in your life, with his focus being on the people closest to you.

> *Jesus said to them, "A prophet is not without honor except in his own town, among his relatives and in his own home (Mark 6:4)."*

When it's up close and personal, not only do we hold on to it longer, but it has a deeper impact. When Satan uses a loved one, someone who is *supposed* to love you unconditionally, we hold on sometimes for years. The longer you hold on to rejection the deeper the scars get, and you begin to feel emotionally unstable, many times feeling as if your emotions are homeless, running rampant with no place to rest. You find yourself running in circles mentally day after day, trying to feel good about yourself, all while looking for love and acceptance from others.

My search was never-ending. Trying to love myself was becoming a daily task, so when I could not find love within, my search turned outward. I began searching for a love from people that simply did not exist. When I was unable to find the love I was searching for in people or the love they were giving did not meet my standard of what I believed love should look like, I would run and my search would begin all over again.

I was failing miserably here. As I mentioned before you become unstable. As I look back it's as if Satan was watching my every move, it felt like I was being set up. The more I searched for love outside of God, the more I found myself being rejected. It looked as if Satan was succeeding in his mission, but it also felt like that.

I was being tormented day after day by the spirit of rejection to what seemed like no end. There was no running or hiding from this spirit; I wore it, I packed it up every day and took it with me where ever I went. No matter what happened throughout the day I would turn it inward.

The spirit of rejection had an assignment to fulfill and failing was not an option. Satan was pulling out every trick and scheme possible to keep me bound. This was an ongoing battle and I was losing, I was malfunctioning. The spirit of rejection had not only taken over my life but had become a part of my everyday walk; *"Malfunction causes Dysfunction."*

The spirit of rejection causes you to malfunction, eventually becoming dysfunctional in many areas of your life.

Everything around me felt like rejection, so much so I stopped feeling like I belonged (self-rejection). I felt different. I felt as though I had no place in the world. I was functioning as an outsider and there was nothing anyone could do about it because I was not going to expose myself. The best way for a person with rejection to hide rejection is to deny its very existence.

Talking about it and or exposing myself (in my eyes), would mean outside judgment from the world, and for me that was not an option, so again (in my eyes); I had to hide my feelings and contain my emotions. I could in no way risk people looking at me any other way than what I was presenting on the outside; so internalizing, holding on, and burying everything was my only option, and because of this, I carried this baggage with me everywhere I went.

Not only was rejection fully operational in my life, but it found its way into every relationship in my life, causing them to be unhealthy and dysfunctional as well.

I entered each relationship with rejection, and I left each relationship with rejection. I was broken and shattered entering, and I was broken and shattered leaving.

The person that operates in rejection looks to find healing within each relationship, not realizing that the relationship is just a short- term fix. The truth of the matter is you leave just as damaged as when you came in, if not more. With each relationship you become more broken because the breakdown of the relationship leaves you shattered, feeling as though you've done something wrong, or shall I say, "It makes you feel as if something is wrong with you."

In this state you are not relationship capable, you are relationship handicap.

4

Rejection and Relationships

Shattered and in desperate need of love and acceptance, I begin entering into what I dare not call love, but relationships of acceptance and fulfillment (relationship handicap).

I dedicated this book to every man I've ever dated; to every man I've ever been in any type of relationship with rather good or bad. To the gang member, the cheater, the faithful, to the fathers of my children, and to the ex-husband. Why? Because as stated within the dedication, they didn't have a chance, they were dating the spirit of rejection. I'm in no way excusing their behavior, but what I am saying is that I was severely wounded and unable to function correctly in any type of relationship.

Over the years I believe I have heard from each and every one of them that I was such a good girl, very humble; and I was. What they neglected to see is they were looking at rejection and fear; they were dating a little girl, a fatherless daughter. I hid myself from them; the real Michelle would not dare show up for fear of rejection, because rejection is what I experienced all my life. I was shy and withdrawn, not able to speak up for myself, tolerating any and everything out of fear of abandonment.

The absence of my father caused me to identify every man I have ever dated with him. I would walk in obedience and be the good little girl they expected me to be. I saw men as the authority, *the giant*, the caretaker that my father was supposed to be for me.

My dedication speaks to men because the absence of my father was a hard hit for me and caused me to seek what I was missing from my dad in each and every one of them. I searched and hungered for the validation my dad did not give me in each and every one of them.

In all my humility and being a good girl, if they hurt me at all, or caused the spirit of rejection to arise within me, I would withdraw from the relationship never to return because at that point they had done exactly what I expected them to do; fail at fulfilling my need.

Once I left the relationship there was absolutely no chance of reconciliation, I would never return because of rejection. A second chance; *no way*, as I had now identified them with my past pain and was on the run. Sounds bizarre, but this is exactly what the spirit of rejection causes you to do; run for dear life. Once the relationship was over I was never going to retrace those steps again.

It is next to impossible to be in a healthy relationship when you have a root spirit of rejection, because rejection is always out front. It is not only unhealthy but a health risk for both parties.

Small issues in a relationship become big issues quickly because there is no sensible resolve when rejection is present; it's always about you, and because of this, you either bury the issue or fight your way through it; either way, you find a way to protect yourself.

When I think of healthy, I think of strong, being able to function properly. Healthy to me means being healed. Many times we enter into relationships broken, and then wonder why the relationship is either not working or does not work. Well, here we have our answer; we (some) enter *broken*.

Broken according to Webster's Dictionary means *separated into parts or pieces by being hit, damaged, etc.: not working properly: not kept or honored.* All the above definitions are profound both naturally and spiritually, as rejection affects your life in both realms.

Many people have entered into marriages broken (including myself), not out of love, but a need to be accepted. God honors marriage, but I am in no way convinced that God puts all marriages together.

Therefore what God has joined together, let no one separate (Mark 10:9)."

How many times do we misinterpret this scripture? Consider: 2 Corinthians 6:14 *(Do not be yoked together with unbelievers. For what do righteousness and wickedness have in common? Or what fellowship can light have with darkness?)*

We know and are absolutely sure that if two people want a marriage to work, and this is their prayer and they are willing to put in the work, God will most certainly honor and strengthen that marriage and the healing process will begin, but the way we enter into a relationship is critical to that relationship's survival.

The person that operates in rejection does not wait to be healed; not only do they have an immediate need to be loved, but they need to be covered, they need to hide.

Being in any type of relationship with the spirit of rejection present will cause that relationship to fall apart piece by piece. This is in marriage, ministry, friendship, family, work relationships, etc. Rejection can be very overwhelming for all parties involved.

The spirit of rejection will cause you to do either one of two things or both. It will either demand the full attention of the other party, or it will cause you to withdraw from the relationship altogether out of fear. In both instances the spirit of abandonment is also present.

Rejection causes you to assess each situation that arises in the relationship, while at the same time assessing yourself to see if you can meet the present need. When you feel as though you are failing, fear of abandonment sets in and you begin to prepare yourself for the worst, so running or totally surrendering to the other party (in your eyes) become your only options.

I have come across some great men in my life, but I have also come across some bad ones that I believe Satan sent to keep the spirit of rejection alive and active in me. I would sabotage the good and embrace the bad. The good was unfamiliar, while the bad was familiar; I was accustomed to the bad.

With the bad the spotlight was off me, I had a project, something to fix instead of spending so much time trying to fix me; somebody was worse off than I was. Did I know this at the time? No. The spirit of rejection doesn't allow you to see clearly, everything is distorted. The spirit of rejection was justifying my actions. I was trying to avoid seeing me, while at the same time attempting to be everything I was expected to be in the relationship.

In my attempt at being everything I was expected to be, I always felt as if my back was against the wall. I had to always please, I had to rise to the top of every situation and make it right. It looked like pride, but it wasn't, it looked like control, but it wasn't, it was rejection disguising itself as pride and control.

Pride and control serve as a covering for many ungodly spirits, and a lot of the time we don't even realize that we are operating in it, or that it's attempting to attach itself to us through another spirit. We must remember that dark spirits feed off one another.

I was a high risk where relationships were concerned. If you don't like yourself, how are you going to expect someone else to like you? It's like having a high-risk pregnancy, you have to be closely monitored and stay off your feet or else the baby you're carrying is at risk of being born prematurely or death will occur. This is exactly it; in a relationship you are in a critical state, a crash and burn, life or death situation, so you learn to tread lightly to keep death from occurring. You are unstable emotionally, which causes the relationship to become emotionally unstable.

When operating in rejection, you are not in a relationship with another party; you are in a relationship with your rejection (the spirit of). The other person is only there for the fulfillment of your own personal need; I call them void-fillers. You are simply looking for someone to complete you, to fill a void, that empty space you have within.

In my search for love, I would try and convince myself that I was searching for the right person, which was not the case. I was simply searching for someone to fill a void that I had in my life, all my life, and I came up short every time.

The person that operates in rejection will always settle because they are not whole, they are broken, and every time they fail in their search they fall and become more broken; they get up, piece themselves back together; fall again and break again. It becomes a pattern, they become *repeat offenders*.

Some people when they fall stay down for long periods of time, which is very dangerous because the longer you are down the more you search yourself for fault. Rejection causes you to toil: *to work very hard for a long time; to move slowly and with a lot of effort.* You never stop working to find out what's wrong with you. You make yourself the root cause of every issue, taking responsibility for not only the problem but the solution. The problem here is; in the eyes of rejection, you are the problem, and the solution will always be to fix you. Your thought pattern is distorted and your discernment is off concerning *you!*

Remember you're doing this in the first place because you don't like you, and being alone again is not an option. This is the way rejection causes you to think, which is very unhealthy.

Some women are alone for years because of rejection, because in a relationship they have no idea how to function properly. In a relationship they learn how to sabotage and control. They see their mate as a project in need of their help, which causes the woman to become Jezebelic in nature (spirit of Jezebel); when in actuality her ultimate goal in the relationship is simply to protect herself from harm.

But Naboth told Ahab, "Not on your life! So help me GOD, I'd never sell the family farm to you!" Ahab went home in a black mood, sulking over Naboth the Jezreelite's words, "I'll never turn over my family inheritance to you." He went to bed, stuffed his face in his pillow, and refused to eat. Jezebel his wife came to him. She said, "What's going on? Why are you so out of sorts and refusing to eat?"

He told her, "Because I spoke to Naboth the Jezreelite. I said, 'Give me your vineyard—I'll pay you for it or, if you'd rather, I'll give you another vineyard in exchange.' And he said, 'I'll never give you my vineyard.'"

Jezebel said, "Is this any way for a king of Israel to act? Aren't you the boss? On your feet! Eat! Cheer up! I'll take care of this; I'll get the vineyard of this Naboth the Jezreelite for you (1 Kings 21:3-10) MSG." Emphasis added.

As you see in the above scripture verses, the woman simply takes over and stands in the place of the man. She rises to the head of the family and builds her throne there where she feels safe and in control.

Men on the other hand (some) absolutely must be in a relationship. They need a hiding place; a place in which to hide the insecurity that comes from rejection. They have a need to have their ego stroked; they need to be pampered (mothered).

Rejection causes the man to operate at high levels of insecurity (like Ahab), immaturity and pride. This is where you find the abusive man (some, not all). The abusive man lives within the very heartbeat of his rejection. A woman can never give a man enough love when he has been rejected all of his life, the axe has to be laid to the root and the Blood of Jesus applied.

I have heard a number of men speak of their wives (mates) as being Jezebelic, they speak of her control and her being uncontrollable, but one must remember

Jezebel (spirit of) needs an Ahab (spirit of) to operate effectively.

Spiritual note:

A man can operate with the spirit of Jezebel as well, *dark spirits do not discriminate.*

What is the likely hood that two rejected people will find one another? Very likely. It's like an apple tree. The healthy apples remain and continue to get strong and ready for picking, while the rotten apples fall off the tree one by one, two by two, three by three, etc., and they meet on the ground. The rotten apple does not jump back on the tree to be with the strong, healthy apples, nor does the owner pick them up and place them back on the tree. *Rejection is attracted to rejection,* this way it does not have to experience any more rejection; (the lies Satan tells).

Without the healing power of Jesus, no matter who you marry you will still operate in rejection, the need to be loved will still be there. You will always search your mate for what you need and what they don't have, it is a never-ending cycle.

The only permanent cure for rejection is and will always be *"The Love of God."*

5

I Don't Like What I See
"The War Within"

This is the place where I paused; I paused and took a look back at how I felt about myself and the things that I warred with on a daily basis. Pretending or holding back is not an option for me; the naked truth is the mirror was not my friend because when in it I didn't like what I saw. The mirror was not user-friendly to me. Today it is everything to me, but while walking the grounds of rejection it seemed like hell.

Although I describe the mirror in this way, I stayed in it, cried in it, and talked to God in front of it on a daily basis. Although I didn't like what I saw, I was searching for something good, something I knew was there. This is the place where I chose to search myself, which we know without the power of God is never a good thing. I would cry and cry and cry in front of the mirror because I would see every wound, all the hurt, and all the pain. I would see myself as a little girl all alone in my little space.

Every time I stood in front of the mirror the war within begin. There was always a tugging going on on the inside of me. But what I found interesting in the midst of all the tugging that was going on, is I knew God was there. How did I know? Well, because I believe God was a major player in the war. As Satan was showing me the bad, God was fighting to show me the good, He was fighting against all the hurt and pain; He was fighting to make me whole.

When I looked at myself anywhere, rather in front of the mirror or in the presence of people, I didn't like what I saw or felt. People would try hard to love me, they would compliment me and tell me how beautiful I was, but that's not what I saw, so I would reject the acceptor. I saw only what the spirit of rejection was showing me, that I was unworthy of anybody's love.

I wore my rejection; I dressed myself day after day in self-hatred. This might be a shock for some, but you will be amazed at how many people, men and women alike that can relate to this.

As mentioned above, nobody could change this because in all my hiding I was not going to let anyone get close enough, nor was I going to speak to anyone about it. The mirror was the only place I would address my issues. I would stand in the mirror and break down; my eyes would wale up with tears as I opened my mouth and begin to talk with God. I was never able to say anything good about myself, it was always harsh and hurtful, but I was used to this, my mouth was reciting that which was in my heart.

For as he thinks in his heart, so is he.
"Eat and drink!" he says to you,
But his heart is not with you (Proverbs 23:7). NKJV

As a little girl, I didn't have a mirror, but I had a corner. In that corner, I would sit all alone and think about just how lonely I was. You talk about shooting at and abusing yourself, I did it. I was hard on myself every chance I got.

In all of my achievements throughout life, I would still beat up on myself. No degree, scholarship, blessing, hug, etc. could change this; I did not like what I saw or who I was.

I used my words to abuse myself even when I talked with God. I was always telling Him the bad things about me; what I thought was wrong with me *(I was describing and repeating what the spirit of rejection was showing me).* I'm so sure God's heart was going out to me; I had made myself a *victim of rejection.* I would feel sorry for myself and who I was. I felt as though I had no place in the world.

The victim mentality is very harmful, it chains you to the very spirit that's in operation and tells you you're helpless.

According to Webster's Dictionary, the word victim means *a person who has been attacked, injured, robbed, or killed by someone: a person who is cheated or fooled by someone else: someone or something that is harmed by an unpleasant event (such as an illness or accident).*

When you become a victim to something or someone, you're injured, you're wounded, and you've been handicapped mentally; therefore, as you go through the process of healing and deliverance the spirit of mind control must be broken as well. Your way of thinking must be dealt with because you will only operate within the content of your current mindset.

> *Do not conform to the pattern of this world, but be transformed by the renewing of your mind. Then you will be able to test and approve what God's will is—his good, pleasing and perfect will*
> (Romans 12:2).

Growing up as a middle child was very difficult for me; in that alone, I lost my identity, so this added to the rejection that was already present. I was always searching my home and family for a place, a place where I fit in, but I never found one. I felt as though there was a drought of love in my household growing up, and because of this, I begin to get angry inside the home.

Outside the home I was quiet and a tad bit shy, but inside the home I had become angry and aggressive, so I begin to look for a way out, not just out of the home, but a way out of how I was feeling inside, how I was feeling about me. I was torturing myself day after day, I was turning on myself.

6

Turning on Yourself
"Self Torture"

Year after year, month after month, day after day, and moment after moment it appeared as if Satan was succeeding. I was becoming my own worst enemy. I was spending an enormous amount of time beating up on myself. Satan no longer needed to use people, he had me. I had turned on myself (rejections only mission), I had become my own worst enemy.

When others would beat up on me and do me an injustice, I would turn it inward on myself. I would find myself searching for what I thought was the truth about me. I would ask myself over and over again, *"what did I do to cause this problem and how can I fix it?"* When the truth was, in some cases, I had absolutely nothing to do with it.

When you turn on yourself you begin to take responsibility for things you did not do, you make yourself the problem. In this space, there is torture *(something that causes mental or physical suffering: a very*

45

painful or unpleasant experience). In the eyes of rejection, if you can blame you, you can fix you, and if you can fix you, you can fix the problem.

This is a place where the forgiveness of others seems to come easy, but the truth of the matter is, it's just easier to let it go than to take the chance of feeling rejected by yet another person. So are you really forgiving or are you burying, pushing the hurt down to the very grave of your soul?

Rejection causes you to let everyone off the hook except for you. The danger in this is you're still open to the pain you've endured from that person. Forgiveness is not for the other person, it's for you (forgiveness is a must), but burying issues release bigger issues, which causes you to dress yourself in that pain.

When a person operates in rejection, they turn everything that everyone has done to them on themselves; they become the blame for the actions of others.

I have been used, abused, lied on and talked about, and yet in all this, I would internalize everything, self-torturing myself. When this happens, you chain yourself up and throw yourself in the torture chamber and stay there until you are able to function again.

Satan's mission here is to always make you the culprit no matter what anyone does, and to release the spirit of blame. Remember, rejections only mission is to *"cause you to reject yourself."*

With the spirit of rejection on me, I was unable to defend myself. I could not and would not speak up for myself for fear of more rejection. Addressing people's wrong towards me was out of the question unless I got angry.

The person that operates in rejection will always create a shield for themselves, rather *pride, rebellion, or anger*; they always feel the need to protect themselves from the harm of others. Mine was *anger*.

When I realized I could shield myself with *anger*, I did, and the older I got the angrier I became. It's called a defense mechanism. I thought I had found my solution for my lack of confrontation. I would use my anger as a shield so no-one could hurt me. Of course, this was not the answer, but in my eyes (hurt), it worked.

Satan was having his way; he was at the top of his game. My anger would lead me into confrontations nobody wanted, but this was the only way I knew to defend myself. At this point, I was convinced it was the people and not the spirit.

I learned how to keep myself at a distance from people, I kept myself clothed in anger and I wore it well.

I see this behavior in people with rejection quite often. They clothe themselves in anger, they shield themselves from what they believe to be the source of their feelings of rejection; people. They learn to move quickly into *"I don't care mode,"* in order to avoid a head-on collision with rejection. I get it; you don't want the inner turmoil, you don't want to feel the torture and the mental anguish that rejection causes, so it appears your only way out is to fight.

The problem with the above way of thinking is not only are you dealing with the spirit of rejection, but now the spirit of anger as well, so there is an increase in darkness and the activity thereof.

Most people that have strong spirits of rejection seem to be very humble, loving people, which I believe is their original make-up. Once you get past all the hurt and pain, you will find some of the most loving and caring people you will ever meet.

Amazingly, in this wounded place, I would run as fast as I could into the arms of God for comfort because I had nowhere else to go. Today I understand that running to God and His love for me is how I made it out of the torture chamber. I did not know it then, I just wanted to hide. I wanted to hide from the presence of people, or shall I say what I believed they thought about me. My rejection was reading people's mind and finalizing their thoughts concerning me.

When you see anything through the eyes of darkness, most of the time, if not all of the time you are going to be wrong. In my eyes, everybody was judging me the same way I was judging myself. In this place, the only thing you want to do is to go into hiding.

Most people with rejection live in their own little world rather inside or outside of their homes. It is an internal and ungodly mindset that has control. You come out, then you go back, this is the way you learn to live. You become confined to your own little world. *Back to the Mountain I Go!*

7

Back to the Mountain I Go

A s a little girl from the time I can remember around the age of three years old, I would come out and go back and come out and go back. My mom said I would read a lot, she said I would leave everybody and find my own little space and not talk, I would just read. Today I would say the reading part was a good thing.

Children today are retreating (not a good thing), but they are committing suicide among other things. I understand this because they are dealing with internal issues that they are unable to express. They are looking for freedom from what they believe is a world of rejection. As parents, we must pay close attention to the signs and the child's body language because it speaks and does *NOT LIE*.

My mind wasn't right. Anytime a child feels as if they are unloved by everyone around them, they begin to become emotionally unstable, and you can see this because they become very emotional. They become mentally unstable, unable to see the world as a great place, they misinterpret everything around them. The world and the people in it become scary to the child.

I know this all too well. I was too young to know how to express myself. I would hide and my family would say things like, *"' she's stubborn; 'she's mean;' 'she's evil,' 'just leave her alone.'"* They weren't helping me, but a lot of the time people make an assessment based on what they think they see.

The rejection was getting worse; Satan was using my families' words to feed the spirit. As the spirit was being fed, their words were also growing inside me. I was too young and unable to fight for myself so I was becoming more and more withdrawn, and as their words were taking root, I was becoming the fruit of those very words.

In retreating I would find places to hide both naturally and spiritually (I know this now). These were my mountains. I would come out of the mountain for short periods of time and then return. I did this for years, and as I got older it became easier and easier. I would come out, get tormented by the spirit of rejection and go right back in. I didn't have the strength to stay out too long, I was too scared, and by this time the world had become a giant for me.

People that operate in rejection, are a lot of the time labeled introverts *(world's diagnosis)*, as I was, because they don't like to come out of their shell; but I am in no way convinced that that's God's assessment, nor was it God's assessment concerning me.

The person that has a spirit of rejection has to learn how to function in the outside world once delivered from the spirit. Being social is learned, because spirits of rejection and fear have sent the individual into hiding.

I was uncomfortable when in the presence of people; therefore, I was unable to be in their presence for huge amounts of time for fear of being rejected. I hid because that's what I was used to doing.

As I got older and had children, nothing changed. I would come out of the mountain, but just long enough to be a responsible adult and the mother I needed to be to take care of my children and go right back in. I would make sure I had everything I needed, everything the boys needed and would retreat right back to the mountain. I lived in my own little world.

I made sure my children had their own little playground in their room so they did not have to leave the house, yes; I was training them to be just like me (from generation to generation).

Although I was in the church at this time, I had no idea what I was doing. I needed them to be comfortable in the home because I wasn't going to spend too much time with the outside world.

I felt like Elijah when he was fleeing from the presence of Jezebel *(1 Kings 19)*, I was always running for my life. Like Elijah, God would meet me right there, but I was still running.

By this time fear had a strong presence in my life; fear of the rejection of people had become a stronghold. *Again*, looking on the outside you would never be able to tell it because I had a shield, I was dressed in anger with a little touch of pride.

It took a lot of prayer for me to come out of this place; I had to learn not just how to be social, but to socialize.

When God made the call I was still running to the mountains.

8

The Call

Even with all the above going on in my life, God never forgot about me, and did not neglect to use me. He saw something in me that I was unable to see in myself. God was calling me to ministry and I was running for the life I knew, rooted and grounded in rejection. My gifts and calling were manifesting and my worship was increasing; God was at work, but Satan was too.

There was a war going on and I was in the middle. God was beginning to use me and Satan was continuing to try and abuse me. I met Satan in the pew of the Church and in leadership alike, it was like he was following me to make sure that I continued in the spirit he had spent years developing within me.

I was faithful in the Church by this time, but the truth be told, I'm not one hundred percent sure how I got there. I don't remember anyone inviting me. I didn't grow up in church, so it wasn't like I had been away and had convictions in regards to returning. My only encounter with the Church was around the age of five.

I remember being taken to my grandma's house in Zion, IL (she had 4 grandchildren); being dropped off for short periods of time, at which time she would take me to Church. She would sit me on the front pew, as she was a soloist and needed to watch me.

There was one incident, one Sunday morning that I strongly believe God used to plant seeds of life because it is one I will never forget.

This one particular Sunday morning my grandma took me to Church and she sat me on the front pew which was customary for her to do. She went to the back and came back out in a gold and black choir robe and she begins to sing, but this time it was different, *"she was singing to me."* Something was wrong and she knew it. She also knew that whatever it was, I was unable to express myself to her because I did not know, but I believe she did.

I believe God ministered to her concerning me and chose this particular Sunday for her to minister to my broken and hurting soul through song. This is something that I testify about quite often, as I believe this was the *seed* God used to draw me to Himself. This experience still sits with me today.

I planted the seed, Apollos watered it, but God has been making it grow (1 Corinthians 3:6).

Once I got into the Church I never left no matter what happened or who it happened with, and Satan was in no way pleased with this. God was sending people to water the seed my grandma planted, and He Himself was making it grow. I wish I could tell you how desperate Satan was at this point to keep me in a place where I was malfunctioning, but that's another book.

As I went to Church, I continued to get stronger and stronger in the Lord, and the evidence in that was my refusal to run. I joined the choir (love to sing like my grandma), worked in different ministries and became fluent in the Word of God. I also held cell group ministry in my home, which God used to activate the prophetic call that was upon my life.

I moved non-stop, I loved the Lord deeply and it showed. In all this I was still coming across people Satan was trying to use to keep the spirit of rejection alive and active in me, but I still continued to move non-stop.

Although I was content in doing what I was doing, I begin to have questions that seemed as though no one could answer for me, so I begin to seek God for those answers. I begin asking all sorts of questions in regards to Spiritual things I was seeing and hearing.

The Church I was in at the time did not teach on the gifts of the Spirit and the operation thereof in detail, and because of that, I found myself in the presence of the source; God (right where He wanted me). In this place, I not only found myself asking God questions, but I found that I was a strong worshipper.

One night as I worshiped the Lord for hours in my living room, as I had become so accustomed to doing, I heard the Lord say, *"I have called you minister."* With my hands in the air, I responded, *"What?"* I heard the Lord again say, *"I have called you minister."* I put my hands down, turned off the music and responded to the Lord.

I will never forget it; my response went exactly like this; *"Who?"* *"If everybody else in my life has hurt me, why should I trust you?"* I begin to cry bitterly and fell to the floor. I was devastated. I could not believe what I was hearing. I was satisfied with just going to Church. I was in ministry at Church, I had stayed, and that was enough for me.

I got up off the floor and stomped away angry at God. I moved so quickly that if God would have tried to respond to the uprising of my pain, I would not have heard him. I stomped to my bedroom so out of control that I knocked my open Bible off my nightstand. As I bent down to pick up my Bible, I was quickened by the Holy Spirit to look down at it, as I did, it was opened to the book of Jeremiah, and my eyes went directly to verse twenty-nine eleven.

For I know the plans I have for you," declares the LORD, "plans to prosper you and not to harm you, plans to give you hope and a future (Jeremiah 29:11).

As I read the above verse, I continued to cry. At that moment I heard the Lord say, *"Will you trust me?'* *'Will you give me a chance?"* As I cried my heart softened, and I found myself saying something different. I was telling the Lord *"yes."* I begin to say, *"I'll trust you"* over and over again. I got up and have continued with the Lord every since. Every step of the way God has spoken to me directly about the call at every level, and not to mention, He has never failed to keep His Word.

It's amazing how many people are mad at God and just don't know it. I was angry, and in that anger I had begun to identify God with man; I had snatched Him down off His throne and placed Him at the level of man.

If man had hurt me; *in my eyes*, God was sure to do the same. But through His compassion, love, and patience with me, I found myself singing a new song.

He put a new song in my mouth,
  a hymn of praise to our God.
*Many will see and fear the L*ORD
  and put their trust in him (Psalm 40:3).

Yet in all this I still had my battles to fight, God was still dealing with the effects the spirit of rejection had on my life. I would encounter people that would thank me for a Word released or would speak of my humility in the Lord (couldn't see that).

Leaders would invite me to speak at their churches and/or conferences, some I would and some I wouldn't. When I did accept the invitation to speak at a conference, as soon as it was over, back to the mountain I would go.

The spirit of rejection will always send you back into hiding. It tells you that people have rejected and judged you; it convinces you that people can see right through to your very root.

I want to be clear about something before moving forward. I am a strong believer that spirits transfer and that we should always agree with the Holy Spirit's reveal of things we must be delivered from. It is never wise for someone to be before people trying to bring forth healing and deliverance when they themselves refuse to recognize that they are in need of deliverance. The following scripture verses are a roadmap in regards to the transferring of spirits.

"When an unclean spirit goes out of a man, he goes through dry places, seeking rest, and finds none. Then he says, 'I will return to my house from which I came.' And when he comes, he finds it empty, swept, and put in order. Then he goes and takes with him seven other spirits more wicked than himself, and they enter and dwell there; and the last state of that man is worse than the first. So shall it be with this wicked generation (Matthew 12:43-45)."

As I was going through this process, I always kept view of, and *never* neglected my own deliverance. I knew and understood that I was in the process of being delivered from the spirit of rejection, and I in no way wanted to release that onto the people; therefore, I only moved when God said move.

The conferences I did speak at would turn out great and people would receive all that God had for them. God would completely take over, and not only were the people being healed, but I was too. The Word of the Lord was coming up and out of me, but that same Word was strengthening me.

As I continued in the work of the Lord, He revealed to me that my life was my ministry; with that Word, I surrendered my life to Him to do as He pleased.

At this point, I had begun to speak to the mountain because as long as it was there, I was going to continue to go back to it. As I used to tell my children, I'll tell you as I conclude this chapter; *"use your words,"* they are filled with power and authority.

He replied, "Because you have so little faith. Truly I tell you, if you have faith as small as a mustard seed, you can say to this mountain, 'Move from here to there,' and it will move. Nothing will be impossible for you (Matthew 17:20)."

"Truly I tell you, if anyone says to this mountain, 'Go, throw yourself into the sea,' and does not doubt in their heart but believes that what they say will happen, it will be done for them (Mark 11:23).

9

The "Seat" of Rejection

Throughout the years my relationship with God was increasing the more and more. I started out knowing Him as my creator, the creator of heaven and earth and everything in it, but as He healed and delivered me from my pain, I begin to know and recognize Him as my Father, calling Him Daddy, as I still do today. Our relationship had changed; it had become one of intimacy.

> *I admit I once lived by rumors of you; now I have it all firsthand—from my own eyes and ears! I'm sorry—forgive me. I'll never do that again, I promise! I'll never again live on crusts of hearsay, crumbs of rumor* (Job 42:5-6)." MSG

Calling God daddy is a strong representation of the unconditional love He showered me with throughout my years of healing. Although I was having problems and struggled to believe Him for my healing, He never gave up on me. Even in my darkest of places, He allowed me to crawl up in His presence.

When I could not speak a word to anyone, God remained my present help. I learned to trust Him, to tell Him everything, always. When something was wrong, God was and still is my first stop.

My colleagues used to say, *"When things are bad we never hear from you, but when things are well you stay on our phone."* They were correct, and to this day it's the same way, but there's a method to my madness. From the very day God spoke to me through Jeremiah verse twenty-nine eleven, I have never felt that I needed anyone else's help when trouble would arise. God made a promise to me the day He called me Minister and I have held Him to that promise, *"I have stood in my place of promise and never moved."*

Standing in accountability, *"yes always;"* help, *"NO."* My help comes from the Lord, (*I lift up my eyes to the mountains — where does my help come from? My help comes from the LORD, the Maker of heaven and earth* (Psalms 121:1-2)). If God sends me to someone for help I go, but I must be sent. God will always be my very first stop. I will always seek God before I seek man.

Review the past for me, let us argue the matter together; state the case for your innocence (Isaiah 43:26).

For no matter how many promises God has made,
they are "Yes" in Christ. And so through him, the
"Amen" is spoken by us to the glory of God
(2 Corinthians 1:20).

God has never asked me to change this; therefore I never have.

Back to the mirror, we go

God never ceases to amaze me. I have noticed over the years that whenever God deals with my healing, assignments, elevation, etc., He still sometimes does it in front of a mirror where I can see myself in plain view. This is a constant reminder of who I am in Him, and how He brought me through. I must say in that mirror God still has my full attention.

One morning, approximately a year ago, I was standing in the mirror getting ready for service. I was having quite the morning conversing back and forth with my Daddy (God). As I was speaking with the Lord, He begins to speak with me in regards to beginning to do conferences; he said, *"It's time."*

As the Lord spoke to me about this, He said, *"I'm sending you back to Chicago, you are to start a ministry there."* I was really shocked, as I have never liked

Chicago even when I was living there. I just stood there. I was without words, as I thought I was never going back. I left by the hand of the Lord and thought that was it.

In my leaving, I experienced a tremendous amount of betrayal and from some very close to me. Leaving it all behind and pressing on, I continued to move forward in the Lord, not knowing that approximately seven years later Chicago was a part of that forward movement.

Shocked to my very core without a word, the Lord knew (of course) what I was thinking. I was thinking to myself, *"But Lord you know what I've been through there, you know the rejection I've experienced there."* The Lord then said, **"I sat you in the center of rejection to heal you."** In shock, I said *"WHAT?"* For the second time in my life, my Daddy shocked me. I again said *"WHAT?"* I again heard the Lord say, **"I sat you in the center of rejection to heal you."**

With no understanding, I dared not speak another word, I just listened. God continued, *"I allowed rejection to surround you to teach you how to fight, you had allowed rejection to overtake you, I allowed you to get tired, to come to the end of yourself."*

As God spoke to me, He began to shine the light on His Glorious process. He continued, *"In the center of rejection, you have learned to speak rejections language, you know rejection when you see it and hear it, you know what it takes to come out, I will use this for my Glory, I will use it to set the captives free."* The Lord continued, *"You will travel the world and expose this spirit, many will be free as you do."*

One of the things I love and adore most about God is His ability to be patient with us. It is absolutely profound the way God uses every trial and tribulation and calls it a *"path,"* a path that guides us right into our God-ordained destiny.

Trials and tribulations are not a stop sign for purpose, they are just the opposite; they serve as confirmation that you are moving, that you are growing and maturing in the call and will of God for your life. They are not excuses to lie down; they are signals to get up. They are designed to release the fight in you. The plans God has for our lives are non-negotiable, so you're wasting your time trying to negotiate.

For I know the plans I have for you," declares the LORD, "plans to prosper you and not to harm you, plans to give you hope and a future (Jeremiah 29:11).

If you are going to walk in destiny you must know that God called you to it, you must know that all things are working together for good no matter what it looks like. Getting to the finish line of God's plan for your life has to be your focus and your ultimate goal.

> *And we know that in all things God works for the good of those who love him, who have been called according to his purpose. For those God foreknew he also predestined to be conformed to the image of his Son, that he might be the firstborn among many brothers and sisters. And those he predestined, he also called; those he called, he also justified; those he justified, he also glorified* (Romans 8:28-30).

My answer was *"yes,"* what better person to fulfill the plan God has for my life than me, what better person to send into my destiny than me. No one, absolutely no one can fill my shoes better than me, just like no one can fill your shoes better than you.

After all this, God then took me away in the Spirit into the very process He allowed me to go through in defeating the spirit of rejection; *The identifying process.*

10

The Identifying Process

S tanding in the same spot in the bathroom mirror, as God's voice ceased, He begins to take me away by vision into the very process of deliverance He allowed me to go through over the years.

As I stood there, I saw myself standing in the center of a lot of different spirits. These spirits were shaped like people, but they were not people, they were spirits, they were very dark shadow-like in nature.

As I stood in the center of these spirits, I just looked around me in unbelief. I then begin to recognize each spirit and begin to call each one by name. As I did this they begin to fall and die one by one. It was like having a machine gun in my hand firing non-stop.

While some were dying, I took notice of the fact that others no longer had the strength to move towards me, they seemed to be helpless.

As I continued to call them by name, I watched them weaken; I watched as each spirit lost their power. As they lost power, I gained power, my stance changed. Above I mentioned the machine gun because as I was standing in the center, my stance was like that of a soldier in an army, fully prepared for battle, firing non-stop at the enemy.

The spirits I encountered around me were from the birth canal, through my childhood hurt and pain, through early adulthood. Every age of rejection surrounded me, I knew who and what they were. As I stood there, I continued to identify them, calling out their functions and canceling their assignments against my life.

The strongest of them all was the spirits I received in the birth canal. I had not only encountered rejection, but the spirit of murder and abandonment as well, and throughout my life, they worked together as one cohesive unit to try and destroy me and keep me from my God-given mandate.

The spirit of murder was the strongest, it had come to kill me; when unsuccessful, it attempted to bring destruction to my life at every level.

What a powerful process God took me through. I had learned how to function and live with the spirit of rejection, so God *SAT ME IN THE CENTER OF REJECTION TO HEAL ME.*

Without the identifying process, healing will be next to impossible. You have to be more than willing

70

to see your places of brokenness and allow God to bring healing and deliverance to your soul. God never said it would be easy, but through the Blood of Jesus, He said it would be so.

So if the Son sets you free, you will be free indeed (John 8:36).

Being bound wasn't something I asked for, nor did I bring it upon myself, but at some point wanting to be free became my responsibility. I was in no way responsible for the behavior of others, but I was responsible for mine. Blaming others will never make you free; it will only keep you bound.

One of the most important things I learned as I walked through the process of being healed and delivered from the spirit of rejection, is that *"I had to become the receiver;"* I had to open my heart to God's repeated attempts to show me His unconditional love.

Without receiving the Love of God, you will always have the tree of rejection planted at the root of your life.

It's an ongoing battle, but you can't win the battle unless you enter the war. I wanted to win, so I fought; with every tear, I fought; with every prayer, I fought; with every ounce of my being, I knew God loved me even when I was incapable of loving myself.

There is no amount of hurt or pain that God is unable to heal you from. You don't just have a testimony; *YOU ARE ONE!*

In the same way, let your light shine before others, that they may see your good deeds and glorify your Father in heaven (Matthew 5:16).

Today God uses my experiences for His Glory; through my testimony *chains are being loosed, and jail cells are flying open in the lives of many.* In CHRIST; I WIN, and so do YOU!

They triumphed over him by the blood of the Lamb and by the word of their testimony; they did not love their lives so much as to shrink from death (Revelation 12:11).

Scriptures that *Bring* Emotional Healing

he refreshes my soul. He guides me along the right paths for his name's sake (Psalm 23:3).

The righteous cry out, and the LORD hears them; he delivers them from all their troubles.
The LORD is close to the brokenhearted and saves those who are crushed in spirit (Psalm 34:17-18)

You who sit down in the High God's presence, spend the night in Shaddai's shadow,
Say this: "GOD, you're my refuge. I trust in you and I'm safe!"
That's right—he rescues you from hidden traps, shields you from deadly hazards.
His huge outstretched arms protect you— under them you're perfectly safe; his arms fend off all harm (Psalm 91:1-5). MSG

Praise the LORD, my soul, and forget not all his benefits—
who forgives all your sins and heals all your diseases, (Psalm 103:2-3)

He heals the brokenhearted and binds up their wounds (Psalm 147:3).

Trust in the LORD with all your heart and lean not on your own understanding; in all your ways submit to him, and he will make your paths straight.

Do not be wise in your own eyes; fear the LORD and shun evil. This will bring health to your body and nourishment to your bones (Proverb 3:5-8).

When you pass through the waters, I will be with you;
and when you pass through the rivers, they will not sweep over you.
When you walk through the fire, you will not be burned; the flames will not set you ablaze
(Isaiah 43:2).

But he was pierced for our transgressions, he was crushed for our iniquities; the punishment that brought us peace was on him, and by his wounds we are healed (Isaiah 53:5).

The Spirit of the Sovereign LORD is on me, because the LORD has anointed me to proclaim good news to the poor. He has sent me to bind up the brokenhearted, to proclaim freedom for the captives and release from darkness for the prisoners, to proclaim the year of the LORD's favor and the day of vengeance of our God, to comfort all who mourn, and provide for those who grieve in Zion —

to bestow on them a crown of beauty
    instead of ashes,
the oil of joy
    instead of mourning,
and a garment of praise
    instead of a spirit of despair.
They will be called oaks of righteousness, a planting
of the LORD for the display of his splendor
(Isaiah 61:1-3).

Heal me, LORD, and I will be healed; save me and I
will be saved, for you are the one I praise (Jeremiah
17:2).

For I know the plans I have for you," declares the
LORD, "plans to prosper you and not to harm you,
plans to give you hope and a future
(Jeremiah 29:11).

But I will restore you to health and heal your
wounds,' declares the LORD, (Jeremiah 30:17a).

Jesus went throughout Galilee, teaching in their
synagogues, proclaiming the good news of the
kingdom, and healing every disease and sickness
among the people. News about him spread all over
Syria, and people brought to him all who were ill
with various diseases, those suffering severe pain,
the demon-possessed, those having seizures, and the

paralyzed; and he healed them. Large crowds from Galilee, the Decapolis, Jerusalem, Judea and the region across the Jordan followed him (Matthew 4:23-25).

"Come to me, all you who are weary and burdened, and I will give you rest. Take my yoke upon you and learn from me, for I am gentle and humble in heart, and you will find rest for your souls (Matthew 11:28-29).

*and the people all tried to touch him, because power was coming from him and **healing** them all* (Luke 6:19).

I have told you these things, so that in me you may have peace. In this world you will have trouble. But take heart! I have overcome the world." (John 16:33).

You know what has happened throughout the province of Judea, beginning in Galilee after the baptism that John preached— how God anointed Jesus of Nazareth with the Holy Spirit and power, and how he went around doing good and healing all who were under the power of the devil, because God was with him (Acts 101:37-38).

The Spirit you received does not make you slaves, so that you live in fear again; rather, the Spirit you received brought about your adoption to sonship. And by him we cry, "Abba, Father." The Spirit himself testifies with our spirit that we are God's children (Romans 8:15-16).

In the same way, the Spirit helps us in our weakness. We do not know what we ought to pray for, but the Spirit himself intercedes for us through wordless groans (Romans 8:26).

Praise be to the God and Father of our Lord Jesus Christ, the Father of compassion and the God of all comfort, who comforts us in all our troubles, so that we can comfort those in any trouble with the comfort we ourselves receive from God. For just as we share abundantly in the sufferings of Christ, so also our comfort abounds through Christ. If we are distressed, it is for your comfort and salvation; if we are comforted, it is for your comfort, which produces in you patient endurance of the same sufferings we suffer. And our hope for you is firm, because we know that just as you share in our sufferings, so also you share in our comfort.

We do not want you to be uninformed, brothers and sisters, about the troubles we experienced in the province of Asia. We were under great pressure, far beyond our ability to endure, so that we despaired of life itself (2 Corinthians 1:3-8).

Let the peace of Christ rule in your hearts, since as members of one body you were called to peace. And be thankful (Colossians 3:15).

Submit yourselves, then, to God. Resist the devil, and he will flee from you (James 4:7).

"He himself bore our sins" in his body on the cross, so that we might die to sins and live for righteousness; "by his wounds you have been healed." (1 Peter 2:24).

And Finally:

For God so loved the world that he gave his one and only Son, that whoever believes in him shall not perish but have eternal life (John 3:16).

In Conclusion: I pray that as you have had the opportunity to take a walk in my shoes through the pages of this book, that you would trade yours in for a brand new pair. It has been my pleasure to share my life with you, it has been my pleasure to expose the spirit of rejection, and finally; it has been my pleasure to serve you and be a vessel of the Most High God! Thank you for your time and obedience to the Father in picking up this book.

Apostle Michelle Gibert.

NOW GO WALK IN VICTORY, IT HAS BEEN ASSIGNED TO YOU!

My Personal Notes:

My Personal Prayer:

Complete!

Thank You, Jesus!

Titles by Michelle Gibert

BREAKING DOWN BARRIERS
"THE *KEYS* to UNLOCKING DESTINY"

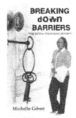

www.amazon.com
(Direct link) www.amazon.com/dp/1548626260

BETRAYAL SATAN'S DEADLY *"HEADLOCK"*
EXPOSED & DEFEATED

www.amazon.com
(Direct Link) www.amazon.com/dp/1726778436

Michelle Gibert is Sr. Pastor and founder of Interceding With The Word Christian Center Intl. (Davie, Fl), ordained and anointed by God through Apostolic and Prophetic ministry. Given strong levels of grace in prophetic, deliverance and wisdom, Michelle has dedicated her life to interceding for others.

Step by step, in God's order and in His timing, God has transitioned her from Disciple to Minister, to Pastor, to Apostle *(Jeremiah 29:11)*. She has been called to release victory in the lives of believers, through the preaching and teaching of the Word of God.

Interceding With The Word Christian Center Intl. is a non-denominational ministry with an apostolic vision to impart, equip, and activate the saints to a new level of warfare, deliverance, and Kingdom living.

God has placed a strong desire in her heart to see men and women everywhere set free from oppression.

Michelle continues to remain thankful that God has ordered her steps and has taken his time with her the entire way. She has declared in her heart and decreed with her mouth that she will serve the Lord all the days of her life.

Made in the USA
Coppell, TX
01 July 2023

18658726R00056